AF746487

Goat on a Trampoline

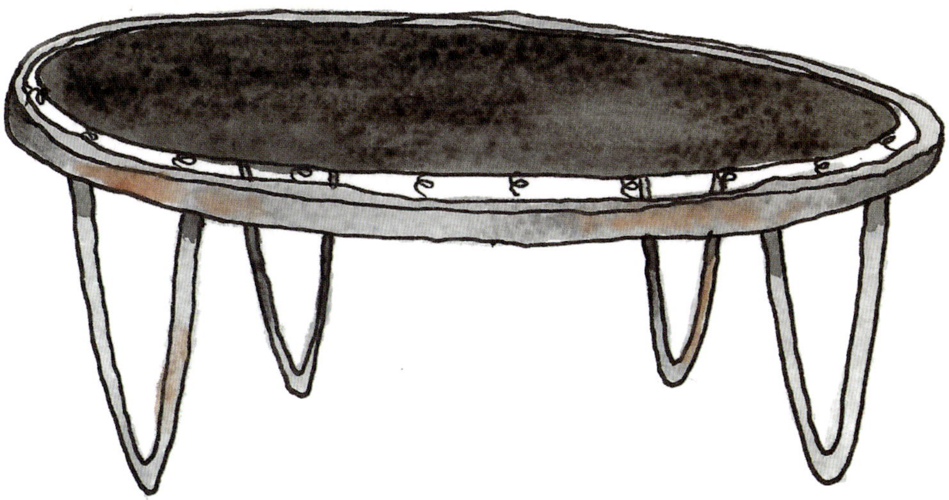

For my kids: Finlay, Josie and Ella x

– Amy

For Macy

– Ross

Goat on a Trampoline

Amy Harrop
Illustrated by Ross Hamilton

BATEMAN BOOKS

Lily Goat was white and lean
and really quite a sassy queen.
But she was bored and she was blue,
she yearned for something new to do.

She'd chewed a jandal
and chased the dog,

disturbed a wētā under a log.

She stole a pav from the windowsill,

and roly-polied down a hill.

She'd tossed a gumboot onto the shed,

and butted the letterbox with her head.

All these things **Lily** had done before.

She longed for adventure, something more.

One afternoon, while squelching mud,

an idea hit her with a **thud.**

She gazed beyond the flax so green,

eyes resting on the trampoline.

The curly springs, the glistening mat:

Lily thought, 'I'll have a go on that!'

Careful not to fall or slip,
she climbed the ladder with steely grip.
Then, stretching out a cautious hoof,
tested the mat for bouncy proof.

A careful jump, a spring, a leap,
Lily landed in a heap.
Back on up, a hop, a bound,
she started bouncing
round and round.

With each jump, her confidence grew.

The higher she bounced, the better the view!

Her goaty hair whipped in the breeze

as **Lily** flew between the trees.

'Hey look,

I'm pretty good!'

she cried,

as the animals gathered by her side.

The next time Farmer Tom went shearing,

Lily began to get more daring.

A spring, a **vault**,

a **loop-de-loop**,

she could glide right through a **hoop**!

Lily worked on her routine,
ensuring each move was crisp and clean.

A half-twist **jump**, a **tuck** then cue,
backwards somersault and **corkscrew!**

The rest of the animals
watched in delight.

This gymnastical goat
was a fabulous sight!

The bull and the duck held up boards with a score,

while the pigs and the horse just watched in awe.

Then **Lily** began to laugh and gloat.
'Have you ever seen such a talented goat?'

She'd bound from only a single hoof
and soar way up above the roof.

She would jump and flip and cry out, **'See!**

You'll never be as great as me!'

The animals turned and walked away,

annoyed at what **Lily** had to say.

Then one day, while she was being cocky,

Lily's routine began to go rocky.

As she leapt up to a half-twist flip,

her cloven feet gave a little slip.

Her horns caught a kōwhai branch up high

and left her dangling in the sky!

Lily shouted out, **'Oh bleat!**

I'm stuck and I can't use my feet!'

The animals all looked up and giggled

as boastful **Lily** writhed and wriggled.

Lily gave a woeful yelp
and begged the others, 'Please will you help?
I know I have been a showy goat.
It was wrong of me to tease and gloat.
Please help me down and I promise you,
I'll apologise and
be nicer too!'

The animals made a farmyard stack,
then poor old **Lily** climbed on their back.
They helped her down, one by one,
until the goat rescue was done.

A humble **Lily** looked in their eyes,
and very sincerely apologised.
She decided after her mistake,
it was time to give the tramp a break.

The next day . . .

Lily was bored and she was blue,

she yearned for something new to do . . .

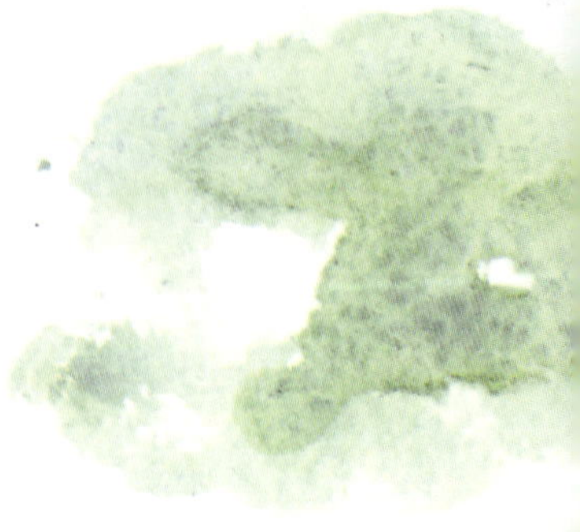

This edition published by David Bateman Ltd, 2022
Unit 2/5 Workspace Drive, Hobsonville,
Auckland 0618, New Zealand
www.batemanbooks.co.nz

ISBN: 978-1-77689-023-1

A catalogue record for this book is available
from the National Library of New Zealand.

Designed by Cheryl Smith
Printed in China by Toppan Leefung Printing Ltd